On the Move

Nina Tsang
Illustrated by Pete Whitehead

Rigby
A Harcourt Achieve Imprint

www.Rigby.com
1-800-531-5015

In the park, I'm finding out
how some things can move about.
I stop to watch as things go by.
They float and fly up in the sky.

Look there!
There goes a kite.
What moves the kite?
What can it be?

3

I feel it
and I hear it blow.
I see things move.
Oh, *I* know!

In the park, I'm finding out
how some things can move about.
I stop to watch as things go by.
They float and fly up in the sky.

Look there!
There goes a leaf.
What moves the leaf?
What can it be?

I feel it
and I hear it blow.
I see things move.
Oh, *I* know!

In the park, I'm finding out
how some things can move about.
I stop to watch as things go by.
They float and fly up in the sky.

Look there!
There goes a flag.
What moves the flag?
What can it be?

I feel it
and I hear it blow.
I see things move.
Oh, *I* know!

I stop to watch as things go by.
They float and fly up in the sky.
I feel the wind. I hear it blow.
The wind makes things go, go, go!

Kites dance, leaves spin,
and flags flap in the sky.
Now I know the wind
is the reason why.

I learned a lot about wind today.
It even blew my hat away.